EASTER SHADOWS
R.U.N. the Way, LLC Children's Book #1

THE BUNNY

THE EGG

THE CROSS

AUTHOR
LINDA D. MILLER

Copyright © 2011 by LINDA D. MILLER

EASTER SHADOWS R.U.N. the Way, LLC Children's Book #1
THE BUNNY THE EGG THE CROSS
by LINDA D. MILLER

Printed in the United States of America

ISBN 9781613790809

All rights reserved solely by the author. The author guarantees all contents are original and do not infringe upon the legal rights of any other person or work. No part of this book may be reproduced in any form without the permission of the author. The views expressed in this book are not necessarily those of the publisher.

Unless otherwise indicated, Bible quotations are taken from the King James Version and the Authorized King James Version, Copyright © 1976 by Thomas Nelson Publishers.

www.xulonpress.com

ACKNOWLEDGEMENTS

First, God receives all the glory for this book. The inspired creativity of Easter Shadows was given in 2009; but the contents of this book did not begin to emerge until the second week in January 2011.

In January 2011, progress of thought begin to happen. Ideas begin to flow; words seemed as though they were being dropped from heaven as rain into my spirit and the book began to take form; until the final product, which you are preparing to read, spiritually and mentally emerged. God in his Omniscience made the manifestation of this Easter book happen. So all praise, thanks and glory is offered up to Him! Amen.

Also, I would like to recognize a few special individuals who supported me in the preparation of this project. The Reverend Karl D. Moore, Pastor of Clarkston First Baptist Church, in Clarkston, Georgia for his spiritual covering, untainted and unwavering faith that promotes the attitude that with God I can do all things (Philippians 4:13). Deacon Howard Evans, who spent countless hours with technological assistance and issues. Deaconess Allison Frazier for her kindness in providing Internet research assistance. Deaconess Trainee Yolanda White for her diligence in the selection of the included graphics. And, last but not least, my first cousin, Mrs. Taleah Hill for her editorial services.

TABLE OF CONTENTS

Introduction
    Shadows vi

Chapter One
    Shadow of the Bunny 7

Chapter Two
    Shadow of the Egg 10

Chapter Three
    Shadow of the Cross 13

Chapter Four
    Easter Speeches 16

Introduction

SHADOWS

Shadows are lurking everywhere
In the shade of a tree in the stuff that we sneeze.
Even in the cool of an evening breeze.

We can see Shadows everywhere!

Shadows show a likeness so you can see what it might bring
And remember shadows are the image of the real thing.

As you continue to read this book
Open your heart and mind and take a shadow look.
Read each story so that you can see
Which shadow will you choose to seek?

Chapter One

SHADOW OF THE BUNNY

~~~

To some, the Bunny is a cute and precious animal that brings warmth to the hearts when it is seen.

Bunnies are fluffy white, fluffy grey or fluffy brown.
They can be seen in the greenery of the grass which is all around.

Vegetables are their food and carrots are a treat.
They help to keep the bunny healthy and neat.

The bunny hops as it plans to travel throughout all the land. Hippity, hoppity all through the day as the bunny watch the children during their Easter play.

It is fun to hop on Easter day. While running and playing in every way. To hop like a bunny we jump back and forth. As we wiggle our noses and listen for noise.

EASTER SHADOWS R.U.N. the Way, LLC Children's Book #1

This is one way we celebrate Easter day like a bunny. Hippity, hop hoppity all the way. **Chasing shadows and acting quite funny.**

The bunnies stretch out their ears sometimes up sometimes down. To clearly hear the things that are all around. Their big floppy ears let them know what is near.

On Easter day they use their ears to listen and hear. All the laughter and the children's Easter cheer.

As they gaze upon the children through the shadows of the trees. **Can someone tell me how does the BUNNY fit into the Easter scene?**

I have not seen a Bunny eat chocolate, not for any reason. It is not a good thing to feed a Bunny chocolate in any season.

It will make their stomach churn, ache and scream! This is surely not a natural thing! **So, how did the BUNNY get into the Easter scene?**

EASTER SHADOWS R.U.N. the Way, LLC Children's Book #1

The sight of a Bunny brings happiness to the hearts of men, women, girls and boys. Just to look upon a fluffy one brings our hearts joy.

Not a shadow of a bunny we see. For we look upon the real thing and this sight gives us glee.

As the bunny begins to hop, hoppity hop. Let us now see where it stops.

Hippity, hop hoppity with its legs. Now the bunny has stopped at the shadow of the egg.

Chapter Two

SHADOW OF THE EGG

~~~

How does an egg hook up with a bunny?

Let us see. If the bunny was hungry maybe the egg it would eat.

Eating of eggs is not a bunny's habit. Remember the bunny eats vegetables and its treat is a carrot.

Maybe the egg rolled out from its care. And found itself just lying there.

In the greenery of a park or in the privacy of a back yard. **Do we know where the Easter Egg really got its start?**

Its image, so close to the ground that we might see. The shadow of an egg that may or may not be.

But on Easter day all the eggs are dressed up to see. Who will find their place of rest at the Easter feast.

They roll out in a parade of bright colors red, yellow, and green. Coloring the Easter ground with a wonderful scene.

So beautiful as they lay all around. As the tinted eggs paint an exciting Easter picture right on the ground. A splash of purple here and a dash of blue there. Brings excitement to the eyes of the children who care.

The eggs are all boiled hot and fresh. The children eat and eat and make a happy Easter eggery mess! At the end of the feast when all have been filled and nothing is said the children are lying in bed with fluffy pillows for their heads. **Now in a whisper, again I say, how did the EGG get to celebrate Easter day?**

All the eggs that the children did not seek lay in a less than fragrant rotten heap.

Now as we continue to read we will see how the next Begotten shadow is the one we should seek.

EASTER SHADOWS R.U.N. the Way, LLC Children's Book #1

Chapter Three

SHADOW OF THE CROSS

Here there are no hopping Bunny or Eggs that have rottened. This last Shadow tells us about God's only Begotten.

The Shadow of the Cross, all cannot see. Your heart must be open with a mind to believe.

High and lifted up He should be lifted on Easter day. Can someone tell me how this Shadow went away?

From the North, South, East and West this is the Shadow that can be seen best. In the ground, at a feast, across the oceans, and down the street.

This is the great Shadow that we all should seek. Can someone tell me how this Shadow became so bleak?

EASTER SHADOWS R.U.N. the Way, LLC Children's Book #1

This Shadow was once placed in the ground and rose in three days. He is the reason for Easter and its praise.

It was a miracle to see Jesus crowned. When God the Father raised him from the ground. Lord of Lord and King of Kings. Jesus is God's Son and the master of everything.

So as we celebrate on Easter day hippity, hoppity all the way. Stooping to pick up an egg of color let us remember Jesus who truly loves us.

Laughing and singing with all joy and glee, Jesus is the Easter message for all to hear and to see.

We have read the Shadow of the Cross…salvation for all to receive. If you desire, open your heart, and truly believe.

Saint John 3:16 (King James Version):
"For God so loved the world, that he gave his only begotten Son, that whosoever believeth in him should not perish, but shall have everlasting life."

As you have read, the Bunny and the Egg are not the real reason for the Easter season even though they have found a place in its story. Remember, the Shadow of the Cross is the truth of Jesus and the only way to heavenly glory!

Happy Resurrection Day!

Chapter Four

EASTER SPEECHES
(Created by the Author)

EASTER SPEECH #1
LOOK INSIDE & SEE

Look inside and see.
Into the heart that really believes.
There lives a Savior so sweet.
On this Easter day.

EASTER SPEECH #2
IN THE PRESENCE OF JESUS

I see myself standing in the presence of Jesus.
He is sharing with me and so many others.
I shout hallelujah and shout with glee.
Because I know the resurrection of Jesus is what Easter really means.
Happy Easter Day!

EASTER SPEECH #3
MAKE A NEW START

Make a new start on Easter day.
Of knowing Jesus in a real special way.
For He is the truth, the life and the way.
Seek to know Jesus on this Easter day.

EASTER SPEECH #4
THE OLD MAN SAID

The young child asked the old man, "Is Jesus Dead?"
Jesus is not dead the old man said.
He is alive and his abode is inside.
Jesus is not dead the old man said.
He went away but he is coming again one day.
Jesus is not dead the old man said.
He is still alive; Just open your heart and let him in.
He will live in your heart and become your Friend.
Happy Easter Day!

EASTER SPEECH #5
TELL THE STORY

Now THAT I know about the Easter glory.
I wonder why so many do not tell the story.
Of a Savior and his glory on Easter day.

I heard about the cross.
Where he died so that none will be lost.
So now my thoughts will not be tossed on Easter day.

What men may have seen as a defeat.
When they witness His nailed hands and feet.
To an old rugged wooden cross.
It seemed as though all was lost.

But God raised his son from the dead.
It was done just as he said.
And now we see King Jesus as the heavenly Head.
Hallelujah! On this Easter Day!

CPSIA information can be obtained at www.ICGtesting.com
224859LV00001B